The Flourishing Family

STUDY GUIDE

A SIX-WEEK GUIDE TO JESUS-CENTERED PARENTING WITH PEACE AND PURPOSE

The Flourishing Family

STUDY GUIDE

DR. DAVID AND AMANDA ERICKSON

TYNDALE
REFRESH®
Think Well. Live Well. Be Well.

Visit Tyndale online at tyndale.com.

Visit Tyndale Refresh online at tyndalerefresh.com.

Visit David and Amanda at flourishinghomesandfamilies.com.

Tyndale, Tyndale's quill logo, *Tyndale Refresh*, and the Tyndale Refresh logo are registered trademarks of Tyndale House Ministries. Tyndale Refresh is a nonfiction imprint of Tyndale House Publishers, Carol Stream, Illinois.

The Flourishing Family Study Guide: A Six-Week Guide to Jesus-Centered Parenting with Peace and Purpose

Cover designed by Sarah Susan Richardson

Published in association with Jenni Burke of Illuminate Literary Agency: www.illuminateliterary.com.

For information about special discounts for bulk purchases, please contact Tyndale House Publishers at csresponse@tyndale.com, or call 1-855-277-9400.

ISBN 978-1-4964-8850-3

Printed in the United States of America

31 30 29 28 27 26 25
7 6 5 4 3 2 1

Contents

THERE IS NO ONE BETTER

TO RAISE YOUR CHILDREN,

TO JOURNEY THROUGH

THIS STORY

THAT GOD IS TELLING,

THAN YOU.

Introduction

When we became parents, we felt ready to train up our two boys in the way they should go. We adored them and celebrated each one's first smile, first step, first word. We prayed for them and read them bedtime Bible stories so they would know how much they were loved by God—and by us, the parents He'd entrusted them to.

No wonder one of the most frustrating—and frankly frightening—discoveries we made over the next few years was the disconnect between the biblical principles that were so important to us and our responses to their increasingly tricky behavior. We wanted to model joy, peace, and kindness, so why were we so often tempted to lash out in irritation, anxiety, and anger? Where we desired gentleness, we were often harsh in both words and actions. We were well aware of God's patience and grace toward us, so why were we so often quick-tempered and reactive? We certainly had good intentions and a good foundation in traditional parenting techniques, so why weren't we parenting with confidence, peace, and joy?

Because the Bible is our source of wisdom for all of life, we resolved to study it apart from our past assumptions and only after asking the Holy Spirit to guide us. We also began to read more widely about child development and the human brain. As we did, we were fascinated to discover that much of what Jesus taught about how to treat others is backed by neuroscience, and it applies to children just as much as adults.

Then in 2019, we founded Flourishing Homes & Families—not because we considered ourselves experts but because we wanted to share what we were learning with other parents. Our workshops and online and personal coaching became ways to interact with thousands of other families who want to nurture their children well and whose goals are similar to ours.

Do you also long to "get it right"? Do you want to encourage your child to become a faithful follower of Jesus but sometimes wonder whether you know how to do that well? If you're anything like the moms and dads we interact with daily, you picked up this study guide because you're looking for solid, proven, and biblically sound parenting advice. We get it. We know your struggle because we've lived it!

We don't claim to have the exact answers for every situation. After all, each family's history, makeup, and priorities are different. Even so, we want to offer some tools, resources, and principles that reflect God's heart and that we've found helpful to parents seeking discernment and kindness as they engage with their kids.

Permission to Do It Imperfectly

I (Amanda) have exactly one study guide to a popular Christian motherhood book that I worked through when my children were toddlers. I recently pulled it off the shelf, half expecting to find a few sentences underlined in the introduction and little else completed. To my surprise, when I flipped through it, I discovered that I'd made it all the way through the second week and most of the third week before I'd abandoned the workbook altogether. The study had come highly recommended, and it contained real-life applications alongside stimulating Bible study. I genuinely wanted to study and discuss the topics with others. But I found it difficult to carve out time to answer all the questions. Hear me well—I wanted to. At that time, motherhood was overwhelming, and I struggled to keep up with laundry, much less answer twenty to twenty-five mostly open-ended questions each week to try to become the mom God wanted me to be!

We recognize that reading *The Flourishing Family* and deciding to finish this book study might feel like a huge commitment. At this stage, you may be struggling to come up with tonight's dinner plans, much less thinking deeply about how your professed theology aligns with your lived theology and how your own childhood experience impacts your parenting choices. It's like your brain has too many tabs open, and you can't find and shut off the one playing "Baby Shark" to silence a little of the excessive noise. Adding a book study to your already loud, busy, and somewhat chaotic life is no small ask of yourself!

Dear reader, you have permission to do this study imperfectly. Whether you're doing this on your own or in a small group, there's no right way to read, study, and reflect on *The Flourishing Family*. Scratch that. The "right" way is the one in which you're able to flourish while you do it. If that means taking twelve weeks instead of six to complete this, do it! If that looks like listening to the audiobook instead of reading the physical book, do that. If it means texting your study leader and saying, "Look, it's been a rough day, and I'm coming tonight because I need the community, but I haven't caught up on the reading," send that message.

This is the parenting book study where you don't have to have all (or any) of the answers.

You don't need to pretend to have it all together. You don't need Pinterest-worthy finger foods and sparkling floors to host a discussion, or eloquent words to share within the conversation to attend your group. You can end your worst parenting day minutes before arriving . . . and you can still contribute to a meaningful discussion.

How to Use This Study Guide

With your busy life in mind, we've done our best to structure this study so that it isn't an added burden, even with permission to do it imperfectly. We want to echo the heart of Jesus when He says,

> Come to me, all you who are weary and burdened, and I will give you rest. Take my yoke upon you and learn from me, for I am gentle and humble in heart, and you will find rest for your souls. For my yoke is easy and my burden is light.
>
> MATTHEW 11:28-30, NIV

Perhaps you aren't able to gather with others for a study right now. That's okay. We will serve as your guides if you're working through it on your own. We hope that you'll find this study encouraging and that you'll feel better equipped with practices that will bring peace and purpose to your parenting.

If you'll be completing the study with a group, you will want to read and pray over the discussion prompts before you meet. However, you don't have to write out answers to each reflection question on your own time. In fact, don't feel the need to fill in all the blank space in this workbook—unless you want to for your own study, or you want to leave a written record of the work Christ's Spirit is doing in you, to look back on later.

If it's possible to do this work in community, we encourage that for two reasons: First, you'll be cultivating a support system of like-minded, similarly focused friends who are on a parenting journey with you. You'll find so much joy, companionship, and peace knowing you have friends in your circle who will love your kids and treat them with honor, respect, and compassion. Second, it provides a space for storytelling. God wired us for story, and hearing one another's anecdotes, whether from childhood or from earlier in the day, is a divine gift for learning and connecting.

As you engage in the sacred work of studying and storytelling together, we cannot overstate the importance for you to be vulnerable—to be seen and known as you are today, with no facades, no glowing skin filters, no tough armor. This study may unlock some old wounds, personal regrets, and sins that need confessing. We challenge you to bring it all to the table, sharing honestly with others as you grow in relationship and holding space for one another and yourself.

Here's what to expect in each session:

Gathering + Growing: You'll start each session by taking stock of where you are: the ups and downs of parenting that week and how you've been applying what you're learning. If you are meeting with a group, this is also a great time to get to know the other participants.

Putting Jesus at the Center: Before you get practical, you need to get personal. That means understanding the infinite worth of every human being. It means appreciating all that Scripture has to teach you about Christ's infinite love and your unending need for Him. In a world that often downplays sin and celebrates rebellion, keeping your eyes on God and His Word will give you the outlook you need to parent with purpose and peace. The questions in this section are designed to get you thinking about the intent and implications of biblical teachings, as well as what Jesus modeled during His time on earth.

Cultivating Connection: This section is designed to help you consider how to apply biblical principles and findings from neuroscience to your day-to-day interactions with your kids. We encourage you to try the activities introduced in these sections and, if you're in a group, to share discoveries you made or questions that came up from the previous week's ideas. This is also the section you may come back to again and again as you seek to parent with growing confidence and peace.

Storing Up Strength for the Journey: Though you're a parent to your children, never forget that you are also God's treasured child. Some weeks what you may need most is encouragement and a reminder that God's wisdom, power, and loving care are available to you. When you come to this section, remember that no action is needed on your part, other than to rest in God's promises.

Parenting Prayer Prompts: Whether you're completing the study on your own or with a group, there is no better way to end each session than to bring your home and family to the Lord and ask Him to show you where you can apply what you're learning in a way that will strengthen your bonds with them. If you're part of a group, you may also want to share specific ways you can pray for one another and your kids.

If you'd like to purchase and stream the videos we created to supplement each session in this study guide, visit tyndalechristianresources.com.

Dear reader, if we had the privilege of sitting across the room from you as you begin session 1, we would look you in the eye and tell you with confidence: There is no one better to raise your children, to journey through this story that God is telling, than you. He chose you, He called you, and He daily indwells you with His Spirit and offers His wisdom, which is gentle, peace-loving, and full of mercy (James 3:17).

We are so proud of you for your willingness to engage in this sacred work, and we are filled with hopeful expectation for what God is doing in your heart and home. You are dearly loved by Him. Your child is deeply loved by Him.

If you will be leading a group through this study, *thank you!* The leader's guide on page 107 was written with you in mind. As we embark on this journey together, may you find hope in the discoveries you make, strength in the vulnerability you tap into, and joy in the stories you are telling. Remember, there is beauty in imperfection, and growth in embracing the messy, chaotic journey of parenthood. You are not alone, dear reader. And though we're not there in person with you, we're cheering you on every step of the way.

Amanda and David

IN THE MIDST OF THE CHAOS
INHERENT TO PARENTING,
JESUS INVITES US
TO BE ANCHORED TO
HIS CARE AND PEACE.

SESSION 1

Choosing a New Way

To get the most out of this session, read the introduction and chapters 1 and 2 of *The Flourishing Family*.

Gathering + Growing

- How peaceful has your parenting felt in the past week? What has been going well, and what has been challenging?

- Think about what you hope to gain from this study. What areas of your parenting journey feel challenging right now? What changes would you like to see in your parenting or family dynamics?

- If you're working through the study in a group, take a few moments for participants to introduce themselves and share about their families. We encourage you to take notes and be intentional to learn the names and ages of each other's children.

Putting Jesus at the Center

Read Mark 10:13-16.

When we think about Jesus being angry, we often picture Him flipping tables in the Temple and driving out the money changers who were exploiting the poor and preventing average, everyday people from coming to God. It's not hard to imagine Him with a clenched jaw and a strong rebuke, is it? Over and over again, we see Jesus boldly confronting those in power who positioned themselves between people and God.

And that's exactly what happens in this story from Mark where we see Jesus angry at His disciples—but this time, the people He was protecting were children. In fact, the only time any of the Gospels explicitly state that Jesus was angry with His closest followers was when they stood between children and Himself. In an ancient culture that dismissed and devalued children, Jesus not only welcomed them, but He also declared that "the kingdom of God belongs to such as these" (verse 14)—the nobodies, the forgotten, the undervalued. It was a radical departure from the status quo.

Today, we face similar societal norms. The vestiges of "children should be seen and not heard" still linger, though much more subtly. Today it looks significantly more like complaints about children not being able to sit still and unrealistic expectations that they will behave with machinelike obedience.

Increasingly common, though, is the idea that as parents, our attention and priorities should revolve around our children. This may sound compelling; after all, they start out fully dependent on us! But without boundaries in place, the natural conclusion to this idea is what essentially becomes a child-centered home.

As followers of Jesus, we are not called to be guided by our child's every whim and wish, nor by our own needs for respect or control. There is a different way. In the face of societal pressures, Jesus stands with us, inviting us to depart from fear-driven or culturally dictated parenting. Through His example, we learn to parent with a transformative love, embracing each child as a unique and precious image bearer of God. As we seek to parent with Jesus at the center of our homes and families, may we find the courage to resist conformity and instead draw inspiration from the countercultural love for children demonstrated by our Savior.

1. Who do you go to when you need parenting advice?

2. In what ways are you seeking to parent differently than your parents, other family members, or friends? How could Jesus' response to the children and their parents influence your own parenting journey?

3. What are some ways we can create environments (at church, at school, etc.) where this countercultural view of children as image bearers can be put into practice?

4. How can we respect the image of God in our children while acknowledging that they are still learning and growing?

5. What would it look like for you to apply the universal ethical principles of Jesus to your parenting? Take time to consider the difference between being a child-centered parent and a Jesus-centered parent.

For further reflection

Consider what these verses have to say about how we are to regard and treat other people—including our children.

> So God created man
> in his own image;
> he created him in the image of God;
> he created them male and female.
>
> GENESIS 1:27

> Whatever you want others to do for you, do also the same for them, for this is the Law and the Prophets.
>
> MATTHEW 7:12

Cultivating Connection

When Jesus took the children in His arms, can't you picture Him smiling at the parents as they either steered or handed their children over to Jesus? Though Mark 10:13-16 gives us no additional details, our sense is that in welcoming the children, Jesus was inviting their parents to draw near to Him too.

The same is true today. In the midst of the chaos inherent to parenting, Jesus invites us to be anchored to His care and peace. Instead of leaving us to seek outward control, He invites us to cultivate inner calm and steadfastness through a reliance on Him. In John 14:27, Jesus promises, "Peace I leave with you. My peace I give to you. I do not give to you as the world gives. Don't let your heart be troubled or fearful." His peace surpasses the fleeting calm derived from external circumstances like well-behaved children or tidy homes. His peace is His presence through the Holy Spirit, even when chaos swirls around us. Jesus remains undisturbed by spills and messes, unruffled by sibling disagreements, and undaunted by our internal struggles. Anchoring ourselves to His faithful, trustworthy, nonanxious presence offers us a peace that emanates from living in the Spirit and allows us to break free from the desire to manipulate and control.

When we're anchored to Christ, we can extend His peace to our children through our interactions with them. Christ's peace assures us that even in the midst of disorder, we can navigate parenting with grace and patience, calmness and purpose, knowing that His unshakable presence is readily available to us.

1. How peaceful does your current parenting feel?

2. Can you remember a time when you prioritized your child's heart transformation over outward peace or compliance, even though it was less convenient? What was that interaction like?

3. How often would you say that a need for outward peace defines your parenting choices?

As we begin to cultivate a theology of parenting that centers on Jesus' Kingdom ethic, we will regard our children with the respect and esteem due to them as individuals bearing the image of God. Just as your children are unique, your family has a distinct role to play in God's Kingdom. By working to discern your family's core values, you can establish guiding principles that shape the character and conduct of your household.

Often informed by Scripture, core family values provide a moral compass for both parents and children. They help define or clarify what we believe to be right and wrong, and what it looks like to live that out as a Jesus-centered family. It may help to think of family values like rumble strips on a highway or bumper pads on a bowling lane. They won't keep you from messing up, but they will help you recognize when you're off course and provide direction back toward your goal.

One of our family's highest values is honor. While many think of it as synonymous with respect, *honor* implies an extra level of esteem and worth. When our two sons give us opportunities to correct their actions or words, our commitment to honor serves as a guide on how we engage with them and our posture toward them as we correct them.

A couple of years ago one of our boys had a very public (read: embarrassing for us as parents) display of disobedience. Admittedly, it took every ounce of Holy Spirit power within us to respond with kindness and honor toward him. But rather than correct him in front of those who bore witness to the incident, we calmly directed him to step outside with us so we could handle the situation privately.

Our values help us stay consistent when making decisions in everyday life, especially in moments of uncertainty. They help us see the bigger picture and our underlying objectives, even when we're not sure how to put those values into practice in a particular situation or don't know the "right" way to respond to our child's behavior.

If you've never taken inventory of your family values, now is the perfect time to do so! Before you reflect on the list of values that follow, take time to think about areas where your lived values are easily identifiable. For example, if your family regularly budgets part of your income for nonprofit humanitarian work or missionary support, generosity may be one of your values. If your family takes frequent action-packed vacations to explore God's creation, you may value adventure. If you prioritize work and responsibilities before play or rest, you may be naturally drawn to value hard work.

Next, look over the list below and begin to identify which values you hope will define your family culture. Keep in mind that there are no right or wrong answers here. One family may value integrity, respect, and rest, and another may prioritize kindness, service, and fun. Neither family has a "better" list of values than the other, nor is either list morally superior! They each have the perfect values for their family.

- ☐ accountability
- ☐ achievement
- ☐ authenticity
- ☐ balance
- ☐ belonging
- ☐ community
- ☐ compassion
- ☐ connection
- ☐ cooperation
- ☐ courage
- ☐ creativity
- ☐ dependability
- ☐ determination
- ☐ diversity
- ☐ efficiency
- ☐ empathy
- ☐ equality
- ☐ exploration
- ☐ fairness
- ☐ flexibility
- ☐ freedom
- ☐ fun
- ☐ generosity
- ☐ grace
- ☐ hard work
- ☐ harmony
- ☐ integrity
- ☐ joy
- ☐ justice
- ☐ kindness
- ☐ leadership
- ☐ learning

- ☐ loyalty
- ☐ resourcefulness
- ☐ respect
- ☐ responsibility
- ☐ service
- ☐ simplicity
- ☐ stewardship
- ☐ unity
- ☐ ____________________
- ☐ ____________________

This list is in no way comprehensive! You can find many other core values suggestions online. If, for some reason, these fall short in helping identify and clarify your own core values, please take time to look at other resources and get a more robust set of values to ponder and pray over. What matters most is not the words themselves but that you have a clear view of what's important to your unique family.

There's no one right way to explore, identify, and define your family values! The process of discovery is as unique as every family. And as we grow and mature, some of our values may shift and change—that's a normal part of life!

Here is a general guide to help you narrow down the choices so you can begin to focus on what's most important to you and your family:

- Go over the list of values again.
- Choose the fifteen values that resonate most with you.
- Pair any that go together (like empathy and compassion or harmony and unity).
- From each pair, take time to pray over, discuss, and discover which one aligns with your beliefs and resonates with your personality the most. How are they different? Which one most closely represents your values?
- Now you're ready to record your family values. Turn to page 21 and write down your top three values first.
- Next, round out your top five by adding the next two most important values.
- Finally, narrow your focus by filling in the next five core values so that you have a list of ten.

The ________________ Family's Core Values

1.

2.

3.

4.

5.

6.

7.

8.

9.

10.

As you consider your values, consider these questions as well:

4. Take a few moments to think of one personal value you hold. Have you verbally stated it to your children? If so, does your discipline support and reinforce that value or undermine it? Explain.

5. When you think about having a lasting family identity and trust-based relationships, what one core value do you hope defines your family in five years? Ten years? Twenty years?

6. What is one thing you need to change in your parenting (whether discipline or something else) in order to align your actions more closely with your stated values?

Storing Up Strength for the Journey

Give all your worries and cares to God, for he cares about you.

1 PETER 5:7, NLT

Sometimes it helps to remember that you are not just a parent. You are also God's child. Even when you are an imperfect parent, God still remains a perfect Father to you. He loves you with an unshakable love that does not depend on how well the day went. He is not heaping guilt and shame on you. Rather, He is patient and compassionate toward you, abounding in mercy. He is always with you, ready to help you as you seek peace in your parenting.

Parenting Prayer Prompts

Below are some prompts to help guide your prayer time. Feel free to modify them to best fit your needs or the needs of your group.

Praise God for your children and the privilege you have to parent them.

Think about your interactions with your children over the last few days. Confess any ways that you have not treated your children with Christlike love.

Ask the Holy Spirit to help you walk closely with Him and give you His gift of inner peace so that you can approach your children from this posture in difficult moments.

Praise God for His grace, forgiveness, and presence with you in your parenting journey.

Ask God to lead you as you seek to serve His Kingdom by reflecting His character through your unique family values.

NOTES & REFLECTIONS

Use these blank pages to take notes and reflect on this session.

TRUSTING GOD WITH YOUR CHILDREN AND THEIR FUTURES GIVES YOU THE FREEDOM TO TRY A NEW WAY OF PARENTING THAT PRIORITIZES RADICAL LOVE OVER COMPLIANCE AND CONTROL.

SESSION 2

Love over Fear

To get the most out of this session, read chapters 3 and 4 of *The Flourishing Family*.

Gathering + Growing

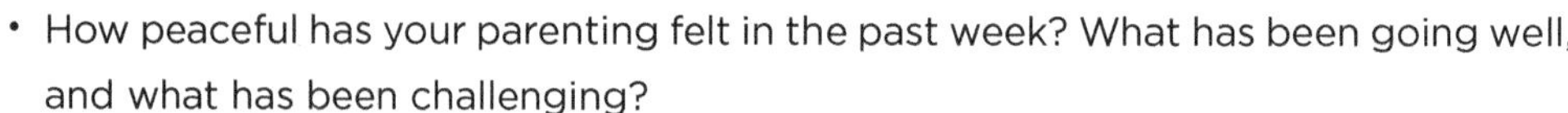

- How peaceful has your parenting felt in the past week? What has been going well, and what has been challenging?

- Have you started to think about your parenting any differently since completing the last session? If so, how?

- Share one "win" from the past week, no matter how big or small. Take time to celebrate and honor the good work Jesus is doing in your heart, home, and family.

Putting Jesus at the Center

Read Luke 15:11-32.

In the parable of the good, good father, Jesus teaches us about the heart of our heavenly Father. This story features a father who ignores societal expectations in the most unexpected and surprising ways. One thing shines through very clearly—his love for his sons. The Prodigal Son could not lose his father's love by his reprehensible behavior, and the older son could not earn his father's love by his excellent behavior. The father's love is a constant, even as the sons struggle to accept it.

1. In what ways does the father act counterculturally in responding to his wayward son?

2. What are some similarities between how the father acts toward his rebellious son and how he acts toward his older son?

3. What lessons from this parable might apply to your own parenting journey?

As parents, even though our love for our children is imperfect, that doesn't mean we can't give them glimpses of the constant, self-sacrificing love God has for them. But when we respond to their bad behavior with anger, harshness, and fear-inducing consequences, we may be subtly telling them that our love could be lost. Or when rewards and affection typically come in response to good behavior, we may be teaching them that our love is conditional. When our love for our children is unearned and unending, we reflect the love of Jesus for them. For it is His love that will ultimately transform our children's hearts.

4. What are some common parenting practices that use fear as a motivator?

5. Consider your own upbringing. To what degree did fear influence how you interacted with your parents?

6. In which situations do you find yourself most tempted to use fear to parent your children?

For further reflection

Consider how the theme of this verse connects to the parable of the good, good father and what implications it could have for your parenting decisions.

> There is no fear in love; instead, perfect love drives out fear, because fear involves punishment. So the one who fears is not complete in love.
>
> 1 JOHN 4:18

Cultivating Connection

Whether we're triggered and stressed out by our children's behavior or trying to teach them what not to do, relying on punishments and negative consequences can actually be counterproductive to our goals. Fear-based consequences can trigger a primal fight, flight, freeze, or fawn response in a child's brain, which can result in a change in their outward actions. While many of us are familiar with the fight response, the other three survival instincts are more difficult to recognize since they often lead to behaviors that look like compliance. Outwardly, our children may stop unwanted behavior, but the fact is, the stress responses that fear causes may hamper the learning of important lessons that will help them do better or different in the future. When in a state of perceived danger and threat, the brain struggles to absorb the lessons we intend to teach.

Parenting with peace and purpose means that we, as parents, work to actively choose not to rely on negative reinforcements. Yes, it may take longer to minimize the unwanted behavior! But take heart: Learning takes time, and trust is something that must be cultivated on a regular basis.

Let's dig in to understand our patterns of stress together:

1. In what kinds of parenting situations do you experience high levels of stress?

2. What are the dangers of responding to your children in the middle of a stress cycle?

Do you know how to calm your body when you start to feel stressed?

In the chaos of parenting, it's easy to lose control of your emotions and then act impulsively as a result. Thankfully, God is not fretting over the messes in your home and is not triggered by your young, immature children acting like children. While this truth may be transformative to your spirit, it takes much strength and practice to cultivate inner calm under pressure. You can learn to control your own responses by paying attention to warning signs that your body is starting to hold stress, including

- difficulty focusing
- tightening of the neck, shoulders, or lower back
- shallow breathing
- feeling snappy and overly fidgety
- checking out
- clenching of the hands or jaw
- sensitivity to touch or noise

It's important to respond intentionally when you start noticing these early signs of dysregulation in your body. These signs signal that your body has begun a stress response cycle. The four practices below (covered more thoroughly on pages 50–54 of *The Flourishing Family*) will help you to complete that cycle, calm down, and respond more intentionally to your children.

- big body movement
- mindful breathing and meditation
- social connections
- rest

3. Which of the early signs of dysregulation do you experience most frequently when you encounter stress?

4. Have you ever tried any of the four ideas suggested on page 37 to help regulate your body? If so, were they effective?

5. What other techniques do you use to calm yourself down during challenging situations with your children?

Storing Up Strength for the Journey

I am leaving you with a gift—peace of mind and heart. And the peace I give is a gift the world cannot give. So don't be troubled or afraid.

JOHN 14:27, NLT

When your peace comes from Christ, you can stop trying to find peace through controlling or manipulating circumstances. Instead of using fear to force your kids to act in ways that allow you to feel peaceful, you can rest in the knowledge that God holds your children in His hands. Trusting Him with your children and their futures gives you the freedom to try a new way of parenting that prioritizes radical love over compliance and control.

Parenting Prayer Prompts

Below are some prompts to help guide your prayer time. Feel free to modify them to best fit your needs or the needs of your group.

Praise God for the perfect love and peace He offers you every day.

Confess any ways that you habitually use fear to parent your children.

Praise God for creating your body to respond protectively in times of real danger and stress.

Ask God to help you recognize signs of dysregulation in your body when you are with your children and to equip you with the ability to calm down in those moments.

Ask God to help you trust Him to transform your children's hearts. Thank Him for loving your children more than you do.

NOTES & REFLECTIONS

Use these blank pages to take notes and reflect on this session.

WHEN WE IMPLEMENT JESUS' VIEW OF OBEDIENCE—ONE THAT CULTIVATES A RELATIONSHIP OF DEEP AND ABIDING TRUST—THAT'S WHEN WE SEE THE BEHAVIORAL RESULTS WE'RE LOOKING FOR.

SESSION 3

Trust-Based Obedience

To get the most out of this session,
read chapters 5 and 6 of *The Flourishing Family*.

Gathering + Growing

- How peaceful has your parenting felt in the past week? What has been going well, and what has been challenging?

- In the last session, we discussed ways to complete your stress response cycle and calm down during draining situations with your children. Have you had a recent opportunity to practice those calming techniques? If so, what was the situation and how did it go?

Putting Jesus at the Center

Read Matthew 21:28-32.

While trying to teach some very stubborn religious leaders, Jesus tells the parable of the two sons. Essentially, it's a parable about changing one's mind and following the God of righteousness instead of stubbornly clinging to self-righteousness. But it's more than that. It's about a God who welcomes the imperfect and is willing to cultivate obedience in the midst of disobedience.

When Jesus invited you to "Come, follow me," why did you say yes? What compels you to follow His commands and seek His wisdom, to submit to His Spirit's work in your heart? If you've been following and obeying Jesus for a long time, it may seem like a silly question with an obvious answer. Jesus Himself reveals what the root of obedience should be: love. On the night before His crucifixion, Jesus told His disciples, "If you love me, obey my commandments" (John 14:15, NLT).

When we read about Jesus' closest followers in Matthew's Gospel, we realize that they remained with Jesus because they trusted Him. Lots of other people came to see Jesus' miracles or listen to His teachings. At first, it may have appeared that they said yes to Jesus, but they didn't stay with Him. They may have been infatuated with the spectacle, but they didn't love and trust Jesus enough to follow Him. Surprisingly, tax collectors and prostitutes were among the relatively few who remained with Jesus. They had discovered a Savior who loved them, and they unashamedly followed Him.

1. In the story of the father asking his two sons to go into the vineyard to work, which son's actions does Jesus count as obedience? What does this teach us about how Jesus views obedience?

2. How could this parable shape your expectations related to your children's obedience?

Sometimes we forget the importance of trust as the foundation for our children's obedience. Young children are so completely trusting that we fail to value it! In an effort to teach the good skill of following our direction, we often rush to forcing compliance—that is, we demand and expect *immediate* obedience. In the process, we erode the trust that actually gives our children the confidence and motivation to obey us. When we implement Jesus' view of obedience—one that cultivates a relationship of deep and abiding trust—that's when we see the behavioral results we're looking for.

3. Why do you think obedience often becomes a main goal of child-rearing?

4. What expectations related to obedience existed in your family when you were growing up?

5. How high on your list of priorities for your own children's behavior do you place immediate obedience? Why?

For further reflection

Consider what these verses describe as the responsibility of fathers (and mothers).

> Fathers, do not exasperate your children, so that they won't become discouraged.
>
> COLOSSIANS 3:21

> Fathers, don't stir up anger in your children, but bring them up in the training and instruction of the Lord.
>
> EPHESIANS 6:4

Consider what the following passage has to say about promoting mutual honor, respect, and dignity within families.

> Wives, submit to your husbands as to the Lord, because the husband is the head of the wife as Christ is the head of the church. He is the Savior of the body. Now as the church submits to Christ, so also wives are to submit to their husbands in everything. Husbands, love your wives, just as Christ loved the church and gave himself for her. . . . In the same way, husbands are to love their wives as their own bodies. He who loves his wife loves himself. For no one ever hates his own flesh but provides and cares for it, just as Christ does for the church, since we are members of his body. . . .

> To sum up, each one of you is to love his wife as himself, and the wife is to respect her husband.
>
> EPHESIANS 5:22-25, 28-30, 33

Cultivating Connection

Trust is the key that unlocks genuine, heartfelt obedience. If we're seeking more than external compliance from our children, we must be focused on their hearts, prioritizing connection, attachment, and felt safety so they can confidently trust us and be open to learning obedience. Prioritizing connection before correction fosters this trust.

Why? Because children are designed by God to seek connection with their parents and close caregivers. It is a fundamental need of childhood—so critical, in fact, that many developmental experts believe that connection is as important as food, water, and shelter!

This is why it can be helpful to reframe "attention-seeking behavior" as "connection-seeking behavior." This shift allows us to recognize that often the core need underneath our children's behavior is connection. And once we understand that, we can learn to let go of the parenting tools that compromise our ultimate goal of trust. By investing in genuine connection, we cultivate an environment where obedience flows naturally.

Thankfully, it's never too late to nurture this bond. Your children yearn for connection with you, mirroring our own longing for relationship with God. As we extend grace to them, correcting them with gentleness and kindness, we echo the boundless grace of our Creator.

1. Reflect on the past week. When did you feel most connected with your children? What are the activities or situations that helped facilitate those moments?

2. What barriers to building stronger attachment with your children do you face?

There are several practical steps you can take to help your children be more poised to obey. Consider how you can co-regulate, connect, and communicate with them.

Co-regulate

Before expecting obedience, check that your child's nervous system is calm and regulated. If your child is in a state of dysregulation, you can be a safe presence and help calm their nervous system.

- Sit side by side with your child.
- Take deep breaths, with your exhales longer than your inhales.
- Offer a gentle touch.
- Intentionally soften your face and body.
- Be willing to wait.

Connect

When your child's nervous system is calm and regulated, look for ways to foster meaningful connection.

- Proactively schedule one-on-one times of child-led connection and play for five to fifteen minutes several days per week with each child.
- Smile and be playful in your interactions with your child.
- Validate and empathize with your child's struggles in difficult moments.
- Before giving a directive, enter their world and ask about the activity they're engaged in.

Communicate

When you need to communicate expectations, consider these ideas to help better prepare your child's heart to obey.

- Use a firm but gentle tone (think sturdy, not harsh).
- Offer choices.

- Ask questions.
- Keep the list of nonnegotiables short.
- Find the yes—be clear about what they can do, rather than focusing on what they can't or shouldn't do.

As you work to cultivate these skills, consider the following questions:

3. In what kinds of situations does your child most often experience nervous system dysregulation? Which of the co-regulating ideas from page 53 do you think might be most helpful for your child in those moments?

4. What is one way you can intentionally connect with your child later today or tomorrow?

5. Think about a recurring conflict you have with your child. How could you offer choices or ask questions to communicate your expectations differently next time?

6. Consider the people throughout your life who have been in positions of authority. Who have you joyfully obeyed and received correction from? What about their character or actions made you more open to their direction in your life?

Storing Up Strength for the Journey

If you need wisdom, ask our generous God, and he will give it to you. He will not rebuke you for asking.

JAMES 1:5, NLT

It's easy for our parenting goals to focus on obedience. Yet like a tender shoot growing into a mighty tree, obedience in our children takes time to grow and flourish. Thankfully, our hope isn't in our child's behavior—it is in Jesus!

As you sow the seeds of trust and obedience, know that He delights in giving you wisdom when you ask Him for it. When you're not sure how to respond to disobedience, ask for insight. When demanding immediate obedience sounds tempting but is not necessary, seek His direction. And remember that He is altogether trustworthy.

Parenting Prayer Prompts

Below are some prompts to help guide your prayer time. Feel free to modify them to best fit your needs or the needs of your group.

Praise God for showing "his great love for us by sending Christ to die for us while we were still sinners" (Romans 5:8, NLT).

Confess any ways that you have not parented your children with honor and respect.

Thank the Holy Spirit for His presence with you during challenging parenting moments. Ask Him to fill you with love, joy, peace, patience, kindness, goodness, faithfulness, gentleness, and self-control (see Galatians 5:22-23).

Ask God to help your children desire to obey.

Ask God for wisdom for yourself and your children so you can grow in your trust and honor toward one another.

NOTES & REFLECTIONS

Use these blank pages to take notes and reflect on this session.

OUR RESPONSE TO CONFLICT WITH OUR CHILDREN SHOULD BE CHARACTERIZED BY GRACE AND WISDOM, AIMING NOT TO CONTROL OR DOMINATE BUT TO NURTURE GROWTH AND UNDERSTANDING.

SESSION 4

What to Do with Sin and Conflict

To get the most out of this session, read chapters 7 and 8 of *The Flourishing Family*.

Gathering + Growing

- How peaceful has your parenting felt in the past week? What has been going well, and what has been challenging?

- As you think back on any attempt to co-regulate, connect, or communicate with your child this week, what stands out?

Putting Jesus at the Center

Read Genesis 3:8-24.

It's an oft-repeated observation that parents never have to teach a child how to sin. But there's another truth about our children: We never have to teach them to see and appreciate beauty either. Kids delight in butterflies and flowers, and they notice the beauty in the ordinary, so a slightly sparkly piece of gravel becomes "the prettiest rock in the world!" The image of God is in our children, and we can catch glimpses of that in them.

Yet even though sin is not our core identity, it is still pervasive and has devastating effects for us and our children. One of our most important jobs as humans is helping our children navigate the reality of sin, both in themselves and in others. They are learning about good and evil along with the blessing of choosing good and the pain of choosing sin. As they encounter the reality of their own sins, our goal is to point them toward the forgiveness and freedom that come only from Christ.

1. How does God respond to His children's sin in Genesis 3? How do you see God's grace shining through His words and actions?

2. What lessons does this passage teach about how to respond to your children's misbehavior?

The Bible recognizes that children aren't like adults. If a mature adult were throwing a tantrum, we would label their actions as selfish or sinful. But it's not so simple with our slowly maturing children. Children will be childish—that's not *necessarily* sin. We must constantly ask God for wisdom to know whether our children are acting out of sinful desire or out of immaturity so that we can respond accordingly.

3. What is the difference between sin and immaturity? Should they lead to different parenting responses? If so, in what way?

4. How did your parents respond to your misbehavior as a child? What might you want to emulate? What might you want to do differently?

5. Have you talked about sin with your children? If so, what have you communicated and why? If you haven't, why not? Take a few minutes to brainstorm how you want to talk to your children about sin and consider writing a sample script that you can use as a guide.

For further reflection

Consider how you can help lead your children toward restoration and reconciliation after they've sinned, just as God does for you.

> Do you despise the riches of his kindness, restraint, and patience, not recognizing that God's kindness is intended to lead you to repentance?
>
> ROMANS 2:4

> Brothers and sisters, if someone is overtaken in any wrongdoing, you who are spiritual, restore such a person with a gentle spirit, watching out for yourselves so that you also won't be tempted. Carry one another's burdens; in this way you will fulfill the law of Christ.
>
> GALATIANS 6:1-2

Cultivating Connection

Every human ever born—including each of our children—lives with the consequences of sin, including, most inevitably, conflict. Our children are not immune to experiencing challenging moments of strife; in fact, sometimes it feels like they're masters at creating them!

In these instances, our natural inclination may be to meet their sin with a sinful parenting response of our own, one that seeks to control or that disrespects our children (because that's often easier or more efficient than connecting and correcting).

However, it's crucial to resist this temptation and instead approach them with respect and understanding, guiding them toward reconciliation.

As parents, our role is not to perpetuate discord but to foster peace within the family dynamic. This means leading by example and demonstrating humility, empathy, and a commitment to resolution. Rather than intensifying the situation, we should strive to de-escalate it, offering leadership and support as our children navigate their emotions and conflicts. By doing so, we not only model healthy conflict resolution but also cultivate an environment where our children feel safe, valued, and understood.

In essence, our response to conflict with our children should be characterized by grace and wisdom, aiming not to control or dominate but to nurture growth and understanding. It's through these intentional efforts that we can contribute to the cultivation of peace and harmony within our families, reflecting the transformative power of Jesus and His heart for reconciliation in the face of adversity.

1. Consider your personal parenting triggers. In what moments is it most challenging for you to show respect for your child?

2. Think of a time when you modeled respect for your child during a moment of conflict. What did you say and do? How did it feel?

Choosing respect in moments of conflict is one of the most challenging responsibilities of a parent. The PEACE Plan has been designed to give you the tools to navigate those difficult moments and model honor and Christlike love. Not only is it a helpful guide for you as a parent, but it's also a tangible tool you can teach your children from an early age so they learn how to work through conflict with honor and respect.

- **Pause:** Slow down and take a few deep breaths before responding to your child.
- **Evaluate:** Reflect on your own needs and feelings in this situation and consider what events or influences are impacting your child's behavior.
- **Acknowledge:** Try to understand where your child is coming from. Do they have needs they feel aren't being met? What perspectives might they be lacking? Ask yourself how you can validate and empathize with your child's experience.
- **Collaborate:** Find common ground. Narrate what you see happening in the situation and look for a solution that will address both of your needs.

- **Empower:** Consider what actions you can take to minimize similar situations in the future. Are there boundaries that can be implemented or skills that should be practiced? Does your child have emotional, physical, or sensory needs that can be met proactively?

Here's what this might look like just before your toddler's bedtime. As soon as you mention bath time, your child transforms into an Olympic sprinter and starts running away from you. Rather than threatening or bribing your child just to get them in the bathtub, take a moment to breathe and focus your attention on the nearness of Christ in this moment (**Pause**). Yes, your child is setting a personal record for running up the stairs, and *yes*, that is frustrating! But if your emotions escalate and you feel like you're about to snap, consider what's going on inside you. It's the end of the day, and you're tired and ready for alone time. There's also still the mess in the kitchen to clean up. And what about your future Olympian? He's also exhausted, but his need for connection and felt safety doesn't turn off at 7:00 p.m. Taking these things into consideration (**Evaluate**) affords you a modicum of compassion for yourself and your child.

Recognizing that your little one may be experiencing separation anxiety (which is normal for that age), you switch up your approach. You intentionally choose to make your bedtime routine a deeply connected part of your day. Since your future sprinter has already run up the stairs, you call up to him, "Ready or not, here I come!" and turn his game into hide-and-seek. His giggles signal where he is, but you pretend to not find him until he pops out and says, "Here I am!"

You exaggerate your relief at "finding" him and playfully move toward him for a hug. You then verbalize his perspective and needs. "I wonder if you wish it wasn't bedtime yet? I get that" (**Acknowledge**). You listen as he responds to your statement.

As you both become calmer, you take the lead and invite him to help make choices about bedtime (**Collaborate**). Depending on your child's personality, you might gamify the early parts of your routine, like turning the march to the bathtub into an animal parade. Or if your little runner needs a long time to start winding down, you might offer a "relax-a-bath" with calming Epsom salts and a game of Calm Down Simon Says.

The last part of the PEACE Plan may not happen just then at bedtime. It may happen the next day when you remind your little one that when it's time for bed he can choose between marching in an animal parade or playing Red Light, Green Light all the way to the bathtub. Because it might take him a few times to remember this plan, you practice it during the day when it isn't actually bath time, to help build his "muscle memory" of what to do when it's time to get ready for bed (**Empower**).

3. Which step of the PEACE Plan comes most naturally to you? What is one step that you find challenging?

4. Share any scripts that you have used during difficult parenting moments. For which steps in the PEACE Plan might it be helpful to develop and practice scripts?

5. How easy is it for you to imagine a situation from your child's perspective? What are some things that are important to your child?

6. Reflect on a frequent conflict you have with your child. What is one step you could take to empower your child and work to minimize this particular conflict in the future?

Storing Up Strength for the Journey

We also pray that you will be strengthened with all his glorious power so you will have all the endurance and patience you need. May you be filled with joy, always thanking the Father. He has enabled you to share in the inheritance that belongs to his people, who live in the light.

COLOSSIANS 1:11-12, NLT

As you walk this journey of parenting, remember that you are cherished by God, who has entrusted you with the beautiful responsibility of guiding your children in His ways. Even in moments of challenge and conflict, His grace surrounds you, empowering you with strength and wisdom. Our prayer for you is that you will lean into His promise of endurance and patience, knowing that He walks beside you every step of the way. With gratitude, press on, confident in His provision and the abundant inheritance of love and grace that awaits both you and your children.

Parenting Prayer Prompts

Below are some prompts to help guide your prayer time. Feel free to modify them to best fit your needs or the needs of your group.

Think about the developmental stage of each of your children. Praise God for the joy and wonders of childhood.

Ask God to reveal any parenting triggers that make it difficult for you to respond to your children with honor and respect.

Confess any ways that you have met your child's misbehavior or disrespect with your own.

Thank God that His mercy is always new and available to you and your children.

Ask God for endurance and patience as you seek to bring peace into moments of conflict.

Surrender the heart transformation of your children to God. Ask Him to increase your trust in Him.

NOTES & REFLECTIONS

Use these blank pages to take notes and reflect on this session.

CONSIDER DISCIPLINE IN A NEW LIGHT: DISCIPLESHIP—AS MODELED BY JESUS—WITH RESTORATION, NOT RESTITUTION, AS THE GOAL.

SESSION 5

Discipline as Discipleship

To get the most out of this session,
read chapters 9 and 10 of *The Flourishing Family*.

Gathering + Growing

- How peaceful has your parenting felt in the past week? What has been going well, and what has been challenging?

- What are some of the wonderful qualities and unique giftings you see in each of your children?

- Were you able to introduce the PEACE Plan to your family this past week? If so, how did it go?

A special note

We want to acknowledge that, in this session, we will be discussing a difficult topic—one that often comes with a lot of deeply held convictions and lived experiences. If you are in a group, our prayer is that this will be a place where all are welcome at the proverbial table and that you can hold honest discussions (and sometimes hard conversations) with honor, respect, compassion, and conviction. We encourage you to pray for peace and understanding before you start this session.

Putting Jesus at the Center

Read Hebrews 12:1-13.

After focusing his readers on the endurance modeled by the heroes of our faith and Jesus Himself, the author of Hebrews encourages us to view the Lord's discipline as a sign of His love and His desire to help us grow in righteousness. Christ, the sinless One, modeled how we might bear discipline: "For the joy that lay before him, he endured the cross, despising the shame" (verse 2).

Before His crucifixion, one of the critical things Jesus did was disciple a handful of followers. He knew that they would soon transform the world and share His Good News across the globe. Yet during much of that time, the disciples were poor listeners and obtuse followers. Despite how often they messed up, Jesus never punished them for their failures. Yet He certainly disciplined His disciples.

When we hear the word *discipline*, many of us immediately think of punishment. However, Christlike discipline is built on teaching and training. While punitive methods seem to work in the short run by modifying behavior, those same punishments instill fear in our children and reduce their ability to learn.

1. Why do you think the writer of Hebrews urges us to accept God's discipline?

2. What are your future hopes for your children? Consider what you desire for them ten, twenty, and thirty or more years from now. How are you coaching them in that direction?

Discipline is a critical responsibility of parents, but we don't need to punish our children—we need to coach them. Discipline is not about inflicting pain; it is about training our children for faithfulness. Discipline doesn't focus on the past; it looks toward the future. This is countercultural, even in Christian circles. As children, many of us were punished instead of coached, with Bible verses used to back up the punishment. It can be challenging now as parents to choose to raise our children in a different way, but it is so important.

3. Why is discipline often such a difficult part of parenting?

4. Do you believe that discipline must be painful to be effective? Why or why not?

For further reflection

Consider what these verses have to say about the role of parents in helping train their children for the Christian life.

> Do not despise the LORD's instruction, my son,
> and do not loathe his discipline;
> for the LORD disciplines the one he loves,
> just as a father disciplines the son in whom he delights.
>
> PROVERBS 3:11-12

> Fathers, don't stir up anger in your children, but bring them up in the training and instruction of the Lord.
>
> EPHESIANS 6:4

> Remember the earlier days when, after you had been enlightened, you endured a hard struggle with sufferings. Sometimes you were publicly exposed to taunts and afflictions, and at other times you were companions of those who were treated that way. For you sympathized with the prisoners and accepted with joy the confiscation of your possessions, because you know that you yourselves have a better and enduring possession. So don't throw away your confidence, which has a great reward. For you need endurance, so that after you have done God's will, you may receive what was promised.
>
> HEBREWS 10:32-36

Cultivating Connection

Several well-known passages in the book of Proverbs are used to justify spanking (Proverbs 13:24; 22:15; 23:13-14; and 29:15). At face value, they do seem to promote this practice. However, when these passages are studied in context, we learn that the "rod" was most likely a wooden stick that was to be used on the back of a severely wayward teenage son as a last-ditch effort to guide him away from destructive behavior that could lead to stoning by the community.

The apostle Paul, who founded and ministered to several early churches, provided a model for discipline as well. After warning the Corinthian church about their prideful divisions, Paul rhetorically asks them, "What do you prefer? Shall I come to you with a rod of discipline, or shall I come in love and with a gentle spirit?" (1 Corinthians 4:21, NIV). We love this question because it indicates that our modern understanding of disciplining "in love" and "with a gentle spirit" did exist in Paul's world. His understanding of a rod and its use stands in opposition to our modern understanding of spanking.

When understood in context, there is nothing in the Bible that commands corporal punishment of children. Also, several studies show that spanking is harmful to a child's development. As a result, dozens of countries prohibit spanking, including many predominantly Christian countries. These facts give us enough reason to pause to consider discipline in a new light: discipleship—as modeled by Jesus—with restoration, not restitution, as the goal. (For a deeper dive and sources on this topic, reread chapter 10 of *The Flourishing Family*.)

1. Were you familiar with the historical context and meaning of the "rod" verses prior to working through this study? What did you learn, or what do you now consider differently?

2. How do you think parents in countries where spanking is prohibited are able to faithfully raise and discipline their children? In many countries, including some parts of the United States, spanking is still common. Why do you think there is such a disparity of understanding and practice?

3. Consider what has informed your personal views on spanking. If you feel comfortable doing so, jot your thoughts below or share them with the group.

Once you move away from spanking and punitive discipline, it's not unusual to feel at a loss as to what to do next. You may find yourself asking, *What does it actually look like to train my children in the Lord and disciple them toward Jesus?*

> As you recalibrate your parenting to a Jesus-centered grace and accountability mindset, we encourage you not to get hung up in all-or-nothing thinking. Rather, shift your thinking to not relying on imposed consequences to change behavior. The goal is for your child to trust your wisdom, guidance, and love, not to fear the consequences you hand down.
>
> *THE FLOURISHING FAMILY*, PAGE 168

We've found three practices to be particularly effective: embracing natural consequences, setting loving limits, and implementing future-facing consequences. The examples below can help you determine which may be right as you seek to help your child grow in various situations.

Natural consequences

These consequences occur without any parental interference and can be powerful teachers over time. The good news is that you can just let them happen and then graciously help your children see the lessons they hold.

Examples:

- When your child doesn't want to carry their pail and shovel to the playground, they may not have anything to play with in the sandbox.
- When your child is kind to a friend's kitten, they may be invited to pet it.

Loving limits

As parents, we must set limits to keep people, animals, and belongings safe. These limits are established lovingly to help our children avoid painful natural consequences. Rather than being punitive and arbitrary, these boundaries are clearly connected to your child's choices and actions in a specific moment.

Examples:

- If your child will not handle a library book carefully, they will have to wait for someone to read it to them, and the book stays on a high shelf.
- If your children can't or won't stop chasing each other inside, they can go outside (or be temporarily separated if going outside isn't an option).

Future-facing consequences

Part of coaching our children is empowering them not to get stuck in habits of misbehavior. This comes through identifying skills or abilities they may be lacking and teaching them during times when they are emotionally regulated.

Examples:

- Play games like Red Light, Green Light and Follow the Leader to help your children strengthen their impulse control and listen closely to directions.
- Have your children create and refer to their own PEACE Plan when they experience sibling conflict.

4. What are some areas in which you desire to see growth in your children? How could natural consequences, loving limits, or future-facing consequences help you nurture them toward that growth?

5. Loving limits can easily become thinly veiled punishments. What is the difference between a limit and a punishment?

6. What is one change or improvement you'd like to make in how you discipline your children?

Storing Up Strength for the Journey

The faithful love of the LORD never ends!
    His mercies never cease.
Great is his faithfulness;
    his mercies begin afresh each morning.

LAMENTATIONS 3:22-23, NLT

Was this a weighty discussion for you? As we delve into discussions about discipline, whether punitive methods or practices viewed through the lens of discipleship, it's natural for emotions like anger, frustration, defensiveness, shame, and guilt to surface.

Yet in Christ, there is no condemnation (Romans 8:1). Thankfully, we are not defined by past mistakes or inherited parenting methods. Jesus walks alongside us, offering unconditional love and fresh mercies with each new day (and sometimes moment by moment). Embrace His faithfulness, releasing the weight of yesterday and stepping forward in faith and trust in His love that endures forever.

Parenting Prayer Prompts

Below are some prompts to help guide your prayer time. Feel free to modify them to best fit your needs or the needs of your group.

Praise God for His unconditional love for you.

Confess any ways you have used punitive discipline with your children.

Receive the grace that is yours in Jesus. Release any feelings of shame or regret to Him.

Ask God for wisdom in training your children to love and serve Him.

Thank God that you are not alone in your parenting. Thank Him for His presence with you in every situation.

NOTES & REFLECTIONS

Use these blank pages to take notes and reflect on this session.

WE CAN WALK WITH OUR CHILDREN THROUGH THE SLOW DEVELOPMENT OF CHRISTLIKE WISDOM, KNOWING THAT GOD'S TIMING IS BETTER THAN OUR OWN AND HIS FAITHFULNESS NEVER ENDS.

SESSION 6

A Legacy of Peace

To get the most out of this session,
read chapters 11 and 12 of *The Flourishing Family*.

Gathering + Growing

- How peaceful has your parenting felt in the past week? What has been going well, and what has been challenging?

- Were you recently able to guide your children by embracing natural consequences, setting loving limits, or implementing future-facing consequences? If so, what was the situation and what did they (and you) learn from the experience?

- What one (or two) thing(s) from this study do you hope to remember or apply in your parenting journey?

Putting Jesus at the Center

Read Ephesians 2:4-10.

Parenting can be wearying. We spend long nights rocking a baby and then late nights waiting for a teenager to return home. Parenting definitely robs us of rest. But we endure so much more than lost sleep. From worries about how fast a baby is growing to anxieties about a child struggling in school to fears about the friends they are making, parenthood can sap you. But we follow a Lord who tells us, "Come to me, all you who are weary and burdened, and I will give you rest" (Matthew 11:28, NIV). In addition, the apostle Paul reminds us that each of our children is a masterpiece (see Ephesians 2:10, NLT), created and dearly loved by Jesus. We have the joy of delighting in our child's uniqueness while knowing that Jesus offers us refreshment when we are worn out.

1. What does this passage from Ephesians say is God's purpose for your children?

2. How could embracing this purpose for them change the way you parent?

3. What holds you back from fully surrendering your children and their futures to God?

Parenting with peace means parenting with trust in God. We believe that He has good plans for our children. We don't have to grasp for short-term behavior modification because we can entrust their futures to God and surrender our attempts to control how they act. We can walk with our children through the slow development of Christlike wisdom, knowing that God's timing is better than our own and His faithfulness never ends. Parenting with the long-term goals in mind can look very messy now. But these may very well be the moments when we're planting seeds for a harvest of wisdom and righteousness in the future. As the apostle Paul reminds us, "Let us not get tired of doing good, for we will reap at the proper time if we don't give up" (Galatians 6:9).

4. Once your children become adults, what do you hope they will feel and remember about their childhood and your parenting?

5. What would it look like to leave a legacy of peace for your children?

For further reflection

Consider how you can help your children develop wisdom and chase after Jesus.

> The wisdom from above is first pure, then peace-loving, gentle, compliant, full of mercy and good fruits, unwavering, without pretense.
>
> JAMES 3:17

> Listen, sons, to a father's discipline,
> and pay attention so that you may gain understanding,
> for I am giving you good instruction.
> Don't abandon my teaching.
> When I was a son with my father,
> tender and precious to my mother,
> he taught me and said,
> "Your heart must hold on to my words.
> Keep my commands and live.
> Get wisdom, get understanding;
> don't forget or turn away from the words from my mouth.
> Don't abandon wisdom, and she will watch over you;
> love her, and she will guard you.
> Wisdom is supreme—so get wisdom.
> And whatever else you get, get understanding."
>
> PROVERBS 4:1-7

Cultivating Connection

One of our greatest desires as parents is that our children's hearts will be turned toward the goodness of God. But following Jesus is more than simply obeying rules; it's about nurturing a relationship with our Creator from whom wisdom flows.

As parents, we play a crucial role in this process. We teach wisdom, not only through words and Scripture but also by allowing our children to learn from their experiences. We understand that their minds are still developing, so we patiently support them as they navigate life's challenges.

Our main responsibility is to ensure our children's physical and emotional well-being as they learn and grow. We provide gentle guidance, unconditional love, and a safe environment in which they can explore and learn.

Our goal isn't to make our children wise overnight. Instead, we aim to nurture their journey toward wisdom, knowing that it's a gradual, even lifelong process and that they will make mistakes along the way. It is in those heavy moments when they've made the unwise choice or behaved in the most unlovable way that we model the heart of the Father for them, demonstrating unwavering, unconditional love that both holds them accountable and restores them without shame.

1. What has helped you grow in wisdom in your own life?

2. Reflect on your parenting practices. Do they show that you value obedience or wisdom more? Why?

We can help our children cultivate wisdom by providing space for them to learn from their experiences. As tempting as it may be to lecture our kids in an attempt to download our adult knowledge to them, wisdom is best learned through trial and error and gradual maturity. There are many practical ways to pave the way for children to develop wisdom.

- **Choose to give a choice:** Children should actively participate in decision-making and be given the gift of experiencing the consequences, both good and bad.
- **Offer small choices within a big boundary:** Help young children strengthen their wisdom "muscles" by offering two choices, such as "Would you rather read a Bible story or a poem before bedtime?"
- **Encourage big choices with small(ish) risks:** Provide a safe space for your children and then encourage risk-taking and creativity within it.
- **Ask questions that lead to the answer:** Open-ended questions can help children problem-solve and come to a decision in the moment or reflect on a wise or unwise choice they have already made.

3. Which of these strategies for cultivating wisdom comes most naturally to you?

4. How comfortable are you with giving your children small and big choices?

5. Share any other practical ways that you encourage your children to cultivate wisdom.

Storing Up Strength for the Journey

Now may the God of peace who brought again from the dead our Lord Jesus, the great shepherd of the sheep, by the blood of the eternal covenant, equip you with everything good that you may do his will, working in us that which is pleasing in his sight, through Jesus Christ, to whom be glory forever and ever. Amen.

HEBREWS 13:20-21, ESV

As you continue on this journey of parenting, remember that the God of peace walks alongside you and dwells within you. Through Jesus, He has equipped you for the task at hand. Like a shepherd, He gently leads those who have young (Isaiah 40:11, NIV). You are deeply loved and cherished by Him. Stay rooted in Jesus, trusting Him every step of the way. With Him as your guide, you can parent with purpose, leaving a legacy of peace for your children to follow.

Parenting Prayer Prompts

Below are some prompts to help guide your prayer time. Feel free to modify them to best fit your needs or the needs of your group.

Praise God for your family and, if you've been studying in a group, for the families represented there. Thank Him for His good plans for your children.

If you've been studying in a group, spend focused time praying for each family. Encourage each parent to share specific prayer requests. Have the group pray for those requests and ask for God's blessing and wisdom for each member of their family.

If you worked through this guide on your own, ask God to help you continue to grow in your parenting and for God's blessing and wisdom for each member of your family.

NOTES & REFLECTIONS

Use these blank pages to take notes and reflect on this session.

Leader's Guide

Studying Scripture and growing in Christ as part of a community are integral to Christian living and the human experience. You understand this and are committed to leading others through this study, and we want to say, "Thank you." Whether you took the initiative and intentionally created this study group, or you unexpectedly took on the responsibility of leading it, we appreciate you. Thank you for being brave and creating a space where parents are welcomed, nurtured, and challenged to grow together.

Participants should come to your group with a copy of this participant's guide and a Bible. We also recommend that members pick up a copy of *The Flourishing Family* so they can explore each topic more deeply.

Before working through each session together, you may want to purchase and download the videos we created to supplement each session. They're available at tyndalechristianresources.com. As you lead, remember that you do not need to have all the answers. Your job is to be curious and kind so that others feel heard and understood when they bring their questions and experiences to the group.

We've envisioned this study to take about an hour, possibly a little more, depending on the size of your group and how eager participants are to share. We trust you to know your group's needs and capacities, but here's how you might plan on structuring each meeting:

- Gathering + Growing: 10 minutes
- Putting Jesus at the Center: 20–25 minutes (including 10-minute video)
- Cultivating Connection: 15 minutes
- Storing Up Strength for the Journey: 5 minutes
- Parenting (Closing) Prayer: 5–10 minutes (This may take a little longer depending on the prayer requests and needs shared by the group.)

Additionally, we've laid out a few recommendations and guidelines on how to facilitate this group:

- Set aside time to prepare and pray for your group each week. We're all busy parents with more responsibilities than hours in the day. For that reason, the sessions are designed to require little advance work. Even so, if you are able to review the questions and preview the video lesson ahead of time, your meetings will run more smoothly. Be sure to pray for participants and their children as well.

- Give each member the freedom to answer or not answer discussion questions. It's okay if they don't have the mental or emotional capacity to respond to each one.

- Allow and tolerate silence. Some of the questions are weighty, and others invite so much vulnerability. Group members may take their time thinking about and answering the questions. Leaving space for silence is encouraged over rushing an answer.

- Set ground rules for your group to ensure that it's a safe place for everyone. At your first session, remind participants how they can cultivate and grow trust through the following:

    » *Active listening:* Be attentive to one another without interrupting or formulating responses while another person is speaking. Listening to understand, rather than to respond, demonstrates respect and fosters trust.

- *Respect for vulnerability:* Honor the courage it takes to share personal stories, struggles, and insights by responding with empathy and consideration.
- *Authentic sharing:* Share your thoughts, feelings, and experiences honestly. Being genuine and transparent builds trust and encourages others to do the same.
- *Confidentiality:* What is shared within the study group should stay within the group, creating a safe space for open and honest dialogue.
- *Empathy and support:* Honor one another's experiences, emotions, and perspectives, and offer encouragement and assistance when needed.
- *Consistency and reliability:* Make your participation a priority. Demonstrating commitment to the group and its members builds trust over time.
- *Respect for boundaries:* Communicate openly about your own boundaries and respect those of others. Respecting personal preferences fosters a sense of safety and trust within the group.
- *Conflict resolution:* Some of the study questions are weighty and a bit controversial. We know that no one wants to confront conflict in the midst of a book study or Bible study, but if disagreement should arise, address it openly and honestly. Show honor and respect for each person, seeking understanding and resolution rather than criticism and condemnation.

As you guide your group through this study, we are cheering you on and praying that God, your heavenly Father, will guide *you* with wisdom, grace, and peace.

A Letter to Pastors

Helping people know and follow God better is what my (David's) life is all about. I suspect it's what your life is all about too. That's why you are a pastor. It's why I was a pastor. It's also why when I had the chance to teach theology at a seminary, I jumped at the opportunity to train others to help people know and follow God. Now the same motivation still gets me up every morning as I lead a Christian college and help young people prepare to do the same thing.

If our goal is to help children and young people know and follow God, then a few years of college or a few hours a week at church aren't going to cut it. The discipleship of the next generation will largely happen in their families. Parents have the key role in training up their children in the nurture and admonition of the Lord. If we're serious about discipling young people, we need to be serious about helping parents.

Yet when I was a pastor, there were few things I wanted to do less than offer parenting advice. If I said anything beyond vague spiritual principles and platitudes, somebody was going to disagree with me. And talking about parenting isn't the same as discussing a more abstract theological topic like the millennial reign of Christ. Parenting is happening in the pews while we preach, and our people are doing it every day. Many have strong opinions about parenting, whether they have children or not! If they have a good relationship with their parents, they often passionately defend how they were raised. If they have a poor relationship with their mom and dad, they may loudly reject how they were parented. Older adults whose children are grown may confidently assert that their parenting methods were definitely the best, while others may speak of their regrets and warn against some of the things they did. Then there are the parents who are deep in the trenches of parenting right now. They're exhausted, they crave answers to their questions, and they really hope their best will be good enough.

I know the trepidation you may have in encouraging a small group or Sunday school class to complete a parenting study that includes topics like dysregulation and disobedience in children, parenting triggers, and godly discipline. There's a chance this study could lead to extra conversations and office visits or, even worse, strained relationships within the church. But there's another prospect—the church can be silent and leave parents grabbing parenting ideas from the wider culture that seem to work. We can deprive parents of the confidence and resources needed to disciple the next generation with Christian ideals at the heart of their parenting.

Consider a third possibility—that you could encourage parents in your church to have meaningful conversations about raising children. They could study the Bible together to reexamine what it means to parent as followers of Jesus. They could even disagree on what faithfulness to God looks like in their respective families and yet still love, honor, and bless each other. Yes, this study may spark some challenging conversations, but when approached with a desire to live out the fruit of the Spirit, these discussions become opportunities to find Spirit-filled unity within our differences.

We wrote this book to help encourage the parents in your church. If there's one thing we want for Christian parents, it's for them to parent in a way that shows Jesus to their children. But that's too hard a task for parents on their own. They need the help of a community. Specifically, they need a church that is willing to walk with them through the joys and challenges of raising children. We hope you will encourage your church to be that kind of community.

About the Authors

David Erickson longs to see God's people recognize that how we live our faith imparts theology to others. Nothing brings this into sharper focus than parenting as our daily lives constantly disciple those who know us best. David previously served as a pastor and spent fourteen years as a theology professor at a Baptist seminary. In 2023 he became president of Jacksonville College, where he guides the faculty and staff in preparing students to lead Jesus-centered lives that transform churches, communities, and the world.

Amanda Erickson is wholly and completely captivated by Jesus. A recovering perfectionist, she has found peace and purpose in the perfect love of Jesus. She's passionate about helping moms be less stressed and angry so they can flourish in their motherhood. This passion was born out of her own experience with postpartum anxiety, rage, and anger. A former foster mom and pastor's wife, Amanda is an artist with a free spirit and can often be found watercolor painting, sipping coffee on her front porch swing, making up silly songs for her kids and dogs, and hiking the woods near her home in East Texas.